W9-BZD-113

Frogs
and Toads

Trudi Strain Trueit

mc **Marshall Cavendish**
Benchmark
New York

Published by Marshall Cavendish Benchmark
An imprint of Marshall Cavendish Corporation

Website: www.marshallcavendish.us

This publication represents the opinions and views of the author based on Trudi Strain Trueit's personal experience, knowledge, and research. The information in this book serves as a general guide only. The author and publisher have used their best efforts in preparing this book and disclaim liability rising directly and indirectly from the use and application of this book.

Other Marshall Cavendish Offices:
Marshall Cavendish International (Asia) Private Limited, 1 New Industrial Road, Singapore 536196 • Marshall Cavendish International (Thailand) Co Ltd. 253 Asoke, 12th Flr, Sukhumvit 21 Road, Klongtoey Nua, Wattana, Bangkok 10110, Thailand • Marshall Cavendish (Malaysia) Sdn Bhd, Times Subang, Lot 46, Subang Hi-Tech Industrial Park, Batu Tiga, 40000 Shah Alam, Selangor Darul Ehsan, Malaysia

Marshall Cavendish is a trademark of Times Publishing Limited

All websites were available and accurate when this book was sent to press.

Library of Congress Cataloging-in-Publication Data

Trueit, Trudi Strain.
Frogs and toads / by Trudi Strain Trueit.
p. cm. — (Backyard safari)
Includes bibliographical references and index.
Summary: "Identify specific frog and toad species. Explore their behavior, life cycle, mating habits, geographical location, anatomy, enemies, and defenses"—Provided by publisher.
ISBN 978-1-60870-245-9 (print) ISBN 978-1-60870-626-6
1. Anura—Juvenile literature. 2. Anura—Identification—Juvenile literature. I. Title.
QL668.E2T774 2012
597.8—dc22
2010016866

Expert Reader: Andrew R. Blaustein, Professor of Zoology & Director Environmental Sciences Graduate Program, Department of Zoology, Oregon State University, Corvallis

Editor: Christine Florie
Publisher: Michelle Bisson
Art Director: Anahid Hamparian
Series Designer: Alicia Mikles

Photo research by Marybeth Kavanagh

Cover photo by *Gary Meszaros/Visuals Unlimited/Getty Images*
The photographs in this book are used by permission and through the courtesy of: *Alamy*: First Light, 4; Phil Degginger, 5 (right); Universal Images Group Limited, 7; Marvin Dembinsky Photo Associates, 20; *Getty Images*: Gary Meszaros/Visuals Unlimited, 5 (left), 21A, 27; George Grall/National Geographic, 9 (top); Panoramic Images, 22B; *SuperStock*: All Canada Photos, 8 (top), 15, 21D, 21E, 22C, 22D, 23B, 23D; Kevin Snair, 8 (bottom), age fotostock, 9 (bottom), 11, 22A, 23A; Cusp, 10; Gary Neil Corbett, 21C; Emi Allen, 23C; *Photo Researchers, Inc.*: James H. Robinson, 12; *BigStockPhoto*: 13A, 13B; *Cutcaster*: Miro Kovacevic, 13C; Ivan Montero, 13D; Sergey Skryl, 13E; Sergej Razvodovskij, 13F; *PhotoEdit Inc.*: Myrleen Pearson, 16; *The Image Works*: Jim West, 17; Journal-Courier/ Steve Warmowski, 25; TopFoto/Mitchell, 28; *Visuals Unlimited, Inc.*: Michael Redmer, 21B; *Animals Animals*: M. Hamblin/OSF, 26

Printed in Malaysia (T)
1 3 5 6 4 2

Contents

Introduction

Have you ever watched baby spiders hatch from a silky egg sac? Or seen a butterfly sip nectar from a flower? If you have, you know how wonderful it is to discover nature for yourself. Each book in the Backyard Safari series takes you step-by-step on an easy outdoor adventure, then helps you identify the animals you've found. You'll also learn ways to attract, observe, and protect these valuable creatures. As you read, be on the lookout for the Safari Tips and Trek Talk facts sprinkled throughout the book. Ready? The fun starts just steps from your back door.

ONE
Frog World

Frogs have been swimming, jumping, and crawling on Earth since before the age of the dinosaurs. They live on every continent except Antarctica. You can find frogs in a steamy rain forest, on a chilly mountain slope and, most likely, in a pond near you!

You probably think it's easy to tell the difference between a frog and a toad. Frogs have slim bodies and smooth, moist skin. They have long back legs for climbing or hopping. Toads, on the other hand, have chubby bodies and dry, warty skin. They have short back legs and usually walk. But did you know toads are actually a type of frog? It can be a bit confusing.

Though frogs and toads look similar, they have some differences.
How many can you find between this pickerel frog (left) and American toad (right)?

Scientists define slim frogs that hop or climb as "true frogs." They use the more general term "frog" to refer to all true frogs and toads as a group. In this book we'll do the same. Of course, sometimes telling a true frog from a toad isn't so easy. Some true frogs have toadlike features, such as bumpy skin, while some toads have true froglike characteristics. Identifying frogs can be tricky, but the more you know about them, the easier it will be!

Trek Talk
Some frogs can leap up to ten times their body length!

It's Not Easy Being Green (or Brown or Gray)

Frogs belong to a group of animals called **amphibians** (am-FIB-ee-uhns). The word means "both lives." An amphibian is able to live both in the water and on land. Most frogs go through three stages of life: egg, **larva**, and adult. Life begins when a female frog lays her eggs in or near water. Depending on the frog, she may lay a single egg or tens of thousands. The eggs are laid in clusters or long chains inside a protective jelly. Some eggs hatch within a few days. Others may take weeks. When **predators** lurk, only a few offspring will survive.

When a frog egg hatches, what comes out looks more like a fish than a frog. A frog larva, called a tadpole or pollywog, has fins, gills, and a tail.

The tiny tadpole feeds on **algae** and plants. It eats constantly! The tadpole needs fuel for **metamorphosis**, the process by which it will change into a frog. Metamorphosis may take weeks, months, or longer.

The American bullfrog, North America's largest frog, spends two years undergoing metamorphosis. First, the tadpole sprouts hind legs. It loses its gills. It grows lungs and front legs, or arms. The tail shrinks. The tadpole stops eating so its horny beak can re-form into a mouth.

Once metamorphosis is complete, the tadpole is an adult frog. Some adults will live in the water. Others will spend much of their lives on land but will live close to water to find food and keep moist. Frogs may live from a few years to more than ten years.

Follow the stages of a frog's life in this illustration.

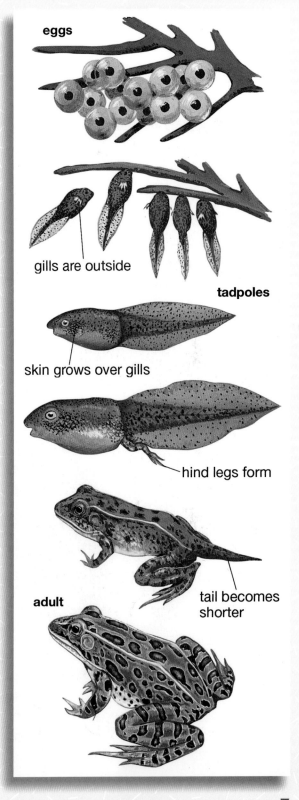

eggs

gills are outside

tadpoles

skin grows over gills

hind legs form

tail becomes shorter

adult

7

Eardrum

Eye

Hind Leg

Fingers

Vocal Sac

Toe Pads

Front Leg

The body parts of frogs help them survive in their watery habitat.

Small Creatures, Big Senses

Trek to a pond on a summer night, and you'll hear a chorus of chirps, whistles, trills, barks, clicks, and croaks. Each type of frog has its own call. Frogs call to find a mate, mark territory, and warn of danger. Male frogs have a vocal sac at the base of the throat. As a frog calls, the pouch inflates like a balloon. The vocal sac makes the noise carry farther. Some frogs can be heard up to a mile away!

Frogs have excellent hearing. They have two external eardrums on the head. Look for a round disk just behind and below each eye.

A male spring peeper's vocal sac inflates as it calls for a mate.

Frogs have two eardrums. They are external and found directly behind each eye.

Sensational Skin

Imagine taking a breath through your skin! True frogs have very thin, absorbent skin. Underwater, a frog breathes by absorbing oxygen through its skin. On land, it takes a drink by sitting in a pond or on wet ground, where the skin soaks up water. The skin dries out easily, so true frogs release mucus and sit in water to keep moist. Toads have thicker skin. They don't lose moisture as quickly as other frogs. Toads are able to live in drier habitats, such as forests and deserts. A true frog sheds its skin about once a week. It wriggles to loosen the skin, then pulls it over its head and eats it for the nutrients!

Big and bulging, frog eyes are located high on their head.

Frogs have sharp eyesight. Set high on the head, their big, bulging eyes can see in all directions. Frogs hunt by sight. When a frog spots **prey**, it flips out a long, sticky tongue, snatches the prey, and swallows it whole. The hunt lasts less than a second! Small frogs dine on insects, spiders, and worms. Large frogs eat small fish, snakes, rodents, baby turtles, and birds.

Trek Talk

Tree frogs are a family with round, sticky pads on the tips of their fingers and toes. These pads work like suction cups to help tree frogs cling to plant stems and leaves.

A frog's body temperature is determined by its environment. It will **bask** in the sun to warm its body. In summer a frog may sit in water or under leaves to stay cool. In winter it may dig a burrow and **hibernate**. The sugar in its bloodstream acts as an antifreeze to keep vital organs working as the rest of the body freezes solid. In the spring the frog thaws, digs out, and hops away!

Now that you've dipped your toes into the soggy world of frogs, let's see them in action.

TWO

You Are the Explorer

In North America, spring, summer, and early fall are good times to go on a frog safari. Pick a day when the temperature is between 50 and 75 degrees Fahrenheit, and it isn't windy or rainy. Take a friend with you. One person can take notes and run the audio recorder while the other snaps photographs. Also, it's wise to leave all pets at home.

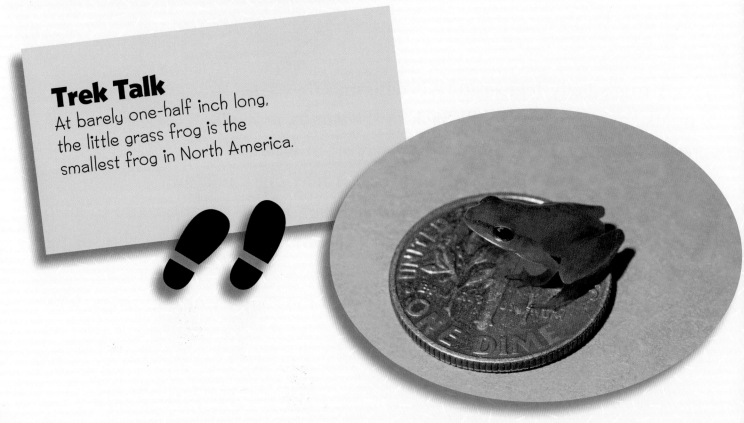

Trek Talk
At barely one-half inch long, the little grass frog is the smallest frog in North America.

What Do I Wear?

* A hat with a brim
* A long-sleeved shirt
* Jeans or long pants
* Waterproof boots
* Sunglasses
* Sunscreen
* Bug repellant

What Do I Take?

* A pair of close-focusing binoculars (4 to 6 feet)
* Digital camera
* Audio recorder
* Flashlight (for an evening safari)
* Notebook
* Colored pens or pencils
* Water to drink

Safari Tip

It's a fairy tale that touching a frog will give you warts. However, there are plenty of other reasons not to handle one. When you pick up a frog, you can wipe off the mucus it releases to keep its skin moist. Touching a frog can put you at risk, too. Frogs naturally carry salmonella bacteria on their skin, which can make you sick. Also, many toads have **parotoid** (puh-RAH-toid) **glands**. When an animal feels threatened, these warty glands (located behind the ears) release a poison. Humans and pets who accidentally swallow the milky fluid may experience burning, nausea, irregular heartbeat and, in rare cases, death.

Where Do I Go?

Frogs will be attracted to these things in your backyard:

* A pond without fish (fish prey on eggs and tadpoles, and they compete with frogs for insects)
* A birdbath, rain barrel, or water feature
* A creek or stream
* A flower bed or vegetable garden
* Anything wet, like a bucket, watering can, or hose cart

If your backyard doesn't offer any of these features, try these locations:

❋ Public ponds without fish
❋ Creeks or streams
❋ Shallow lakes
❋ Wetlands

Always have an adult with you if you are going beyond your backyard. Stay on public property. Also, never wade into water.

What Do I Do?

❋ Listen! You will probably hear a frog long before you see this shy creature. Do you hear a frog calling? Turn on your audio recorder. If you are on a night safari, swing your flashlight toward the sound. Frogs will often freeze in the light, giving you a chance to take a photograph.

Ponds, streams, and lakes are good places to find frogs.

Did You Hear Music?

Do you think all frogs say "ribbit"? Actually, frogs can make some pretty weird noises. They may sound like bells, tools, other animals, and even musical instruments. The American bullfrog's "bwong" mimics the low notes of a bass fiddle. The western chorus frog sounds like fingernails running down a comb. Some frogs are named for their calls, like the spring peeper, which makes a high-pitched "peep, peep"; the bird-voiced frog, which whistles; and the pig frog, which oinks! You can learn frog calls by listening to audio clips online. (Use the resources at the back of this book to find them.) Soon, you'll recognize a frog the moment you hear it. By the way, the "ribbit" frog call Hollywood filmmakers like to use in movies is made by the Pacific tree frog.

❋ Choose a dry, shady spot that's at least 5 feet from the water's edge. If you don't have a pond or stream nearby, settle near a place that gets watered frequently, like a flower bed or vegetable garden. Scan the area with your binoculars from the tops of plants down to the ground. Go slowly. Frogs are good **camouflage** artists. They may even change color while you watch!

❋ Slowly and quietly, walk the area. Look closely at plant stems and leaves. If you hear a splash, stay still. The frightened frog will likely climb back out of the water in a minute or two.

While on safari, be sure to explore plants and leaves carefully for frogs.

Safari Tip

For an evening safari, invite two friends to try this frog-finding technique. Give everyone a flashlight. Spread out so that your group forms a triangle. Position yourselves equally, about 10 feet apart. When a frog calls, each person should shine a flashlight in the direction he or she thinks the sound is coming from. The place where the three beams cross should pinpoint the location of the frog. This technique takes practice. Keep trying if it doesn't work at first!

✳ Snap a photograph or make a sketch with your colored pencils of any frogs you find. Make an entry in your notebook, too. Note the frog's size. Is it smaller or bigger than your thumb? What color is it? Do you see stripes, spots, blotches, or other **field marks**? Does the skin look bumpy or smooth? Does the frog make noise? Where did you see the frog? If you don't know what kind of frog it is, leave a blank line at the bottom to add its name later.

Be sure to take field notes of your findings when on safari.

FROG

Size: bigger than my thumb,
    about 4 inches

Colors: dark green body,
    yellow throat

Field marks: black spots on body

Skin: slightly bumpy

Call: "twang," like broken guitar strings

Location: on grass at edge of pond

Name: _____

> Your Drawing or
> Photo Goes Here

❋ Spend about a half hour to an hour on safari.

❋ Clean up any mess you made, and take all your belongings with you when you leave.

Did you have fun on safari? Don't worry if you didn't find anything. Frog watching takes time, patience, and a bit of luck. At home, upload your photos onto a computer and print them. Move on to the next chapter!

THREE
A Guide to Frogs and Toads

You've had a busy day on safari! Now it's time to identify the frogs you've discovered. Here's how to do it.

❋ Select an entry from your notebook.

❋ If you took a photo, paste it next to its description.

❋ Compare your frog to the photos in the field guide on the following pages. Look at size, body colors, field marks, and skin texture.

❋ If you can make a match, congratulations! Write its name in the space you left in your notebook. If you can't, don't get discouraged. You may still be able to figure out which family your frog belongs to. To help, we've divided the photos into the three most abundant frog families.

- **True frogs:** excellent jumpers that live along the water's edge
- **Tree frogs:** prefer climbing to hopping as they perch on plants near water
- **Toads:** slow walkers found in various habitats, from ponds to grasslands to mountains

Still having trouble? It's no wonder. More than 125 kinds of frogs live in North America—far too many to include here. Also, did you know the same frog can come in different shades and even different colors? Use the resources in the Find Out More section for further help with identification. If you made an audio recording of a frog call, compare it to online clips.

FROG

Size: bigger than my thumb, about 4 inches

Colors: dark green body, yellow throat

Field marks: black spots on body

Skin: slightly bumpy

Call: "twang," like broken guitar strings

Location: on grass at edge of pond

Name: green frog

Frog Guide: True Frogs

Bullfrog

Green Frog

Pickerel Frog

Northern Leopard Frog

Wood Frog

Frog Guide: Tree Frogs

Gray Tree Frog

Green Tree Frog

Spring Peeper

Pacific Tree Frog

Frog Guide: Toads

American Toad

Western Toad

Southern Toad

Great Plains Toad

FOUR
Try This!
Projects You Can Do

Frogs are hearty yet sensitive creatures. These thin-skinned amphibians have much to tell us about the health of our planet. And they are saying that something is wrong. Around the world, frog populations are declining. Habitat destruction, pollution, disease, climate change, the food industry, and the pet trade are some of the things that put frogs at risk. Since the mid–1990s, frogs in U.S. rivers and streams have been turning up with missing or extra limbs. Scientists point to the dumping of prescription drugs, pesticides, fertilizers, and other chemicals into our waterways as a major cause. Experts wonder, if such things are harming frogs, what might they be doing to humans?

What can you do to help frogs? Get involved in efforts to clean up and preserve the waterways and wetlands in your community. Use **organic** pesticides and fertilizers in your yard. Finally, try the projects in this chapter.

Fighting for Frogs in Yosemite

Originally, lakes and streams above 4,000 feet in California's Yosemite National Park were fish-free and frog-friendly. Park visitors could see frogs by the hundreds living along the shorelines. But when people began stocking the park's lakes and rivers with trout in the 1880s, frog populations began dropping. By the time stocking was halted in 1991, three of the area's seven frog species had been wiped out by the fish. Those that remained faced **extinction**. In 2007 the National Park Service began removing non-native fish from six sites within the park. Although 95 percent of the frogs in Yosemite are now gone, it's hoped the program will save the Sierra Nevada yellow-legged frog, the California yellow-legged frog, and the California red-legged frog before it's too late.

One way to help protect frogs and their habitat is to clean the waterways in your region.

Toad House

Give toads a place to take shelter in your backyard. You'll need a clay flowerpot with an 8-inch opening. Choose a shady, damp spot in your garden. Dig a hole about 4 inches deep. Place the pot in the hole, and tip it on its side. Replace the soil in and around the pot so that half of the pot is buried. Place a layer of dead leaves inside the house. Your toad house is now ready for a guest. You can even put a battery-operated light near the toad house to attract insects for your toad to eat. Keep the light within 3 feet of the ground. Be patient. It can take time for a toad to move in.

A toad seeks shelter in a toad house.

Trek Talk

Frogs help control insect populations that damage crops and spread disease. A single frog can gulp down more than one hundred insects every day!

Frog Pond

Attract frogs with a small pond, where they can come to drink and stay moist. Find a 10-inch metal pie tin, plastic plant tray, or clay saucer. Pick a shady spot in your backyard that is protected by plants and out of sight (if you've made a toad house, place the pond nearby). Bury the plate to the rim in the soil. Fill it with about 2 inches of water. Add a flat rock. Replace the water every few days. With any luck, a frog will drop in for a cool dip on a warm day.

Leaves provide a warm place to hibernate for this toad, as well as protection from predators.

Hibernation Station

Here's an easy way to give frogs a warm place to stay or hibernate in cold weather. In the fall choose a 3-foot by 6-foot area among the plants in your yard. Look for a shady, damp spot. It should also be free of all pesticides and fertilizers. Do not cut back plants. Loosen the soil a bit. Spread a few layers of dead leaves over the ground. Frogs will burrow under the leaves, which will act as a blanket during the chilly months ahead. It's as easy as that!

Mysterious transformations. Ever-changing collages of color. Haunting melodies in the night. No wonder frogs fascinate us. These ancient creatures of land and water are, simply, extraordinary.

Glossary

algae	aquatic organisms without roots
amphibians	a group of animals able to live both in water and on land
bask	to lie or sit, enjoying warmth
camouflage	the ability to change skin color to blend in with surroundings
extinction	the state of no longer existing
field marks	spots, stripes, or other distinguishing marks
hibernate	to pass the winter in a sleeplike state
larva	a young frog; also called a tadpole or pollywog
metamorphosis	the process by which an organism undergoes a complete change in structure and form
organic	naturally occurring; without harsh chemicals
parotoid glands	a toad's warty glands that release poison
predators	animals that hunt other animals for food
prey	animals that are hunted for food

Find Out More

Books

Bartlett, Richard D. and Patricia Bartlett. *Guide and Reference to the Amphibians of Western North America (North of Mexico) and Hawaii.* Gainesville, FL: University Press of Florida, 2009.

Bishop, Nic. *Frogs.* New York: Scholastic, 2008.

Elliott, Lang, Carl Gerhardt, and Carlos Davidson. *The Frogs and Toads of North America: A Comprehensive Guide to Their Identification, Behavior, and Calls* with audio CD. New York: Mariner Books, 2009.

DVD

ABC News Nightline, Frogs: What Are They Really Telling Us? ABC News, 2007.

Websites

eNature Field Guide

www.enature.com/fieldguides

Trying to identify a frog? Click on the "Amphibians" link to view photographs and descriptions of North American frogs. You can hear audio clips of the calls of many species, too.

USGS: Northern Prairie Wildlife Research Center

www.npwrc.usgs.gov/resource/herps/amphibid/anura_f.htm

Use this U.S. Geological Survey list of North American frogs to help with identification. Click on each name for a detailed description, photos, and geographic location.

USGS: Patuxent Wildlife Research Center

www.pwrc.usgs.gov/Frogquiz/index.cfm?fuseaction=main.lookup

The Frog Call Look-Up lets you listen to audio clips of North American frogs, from the American bullfrog to the Woodhouse's toad.

Index

Page numbers in **boldface** are illustrations.

Meet the Author

TRUDI STRAIN TRUEIT loves writing about wildlife, weather, and nature. She is the author of more than sixty fiction and nonfiction books for children, including *Caterpillars and Butterflies*, *Spiders*, and *Birds* in the Backyard Safari series. Trueit looks forward to the frog chorus that begins each spring near the creek in her backyard. Once, a Pacific tree frog made its home in her hose cart! A former television news reporter and weather forecaster, Trueit has a bachelor's degree in broadcast journalism. She is married to her college sweetheart, Bill, a high school photography teacher. They live in Everett, Washington. Visit her website at www.truditrueit.com.